Table of Contents

Drinking Rain

Mess of a Storm

June Baby

Chase and Stolen

Harper's song

The Palace

Dear Melissa

Words of Wiseman

The Closing Cover

When the Deaf Sing

To the Man Who Stole the Key

Run Faster Than to Speak

Every Day at 5

One Too Many Ships in the Ocean

The Night I Spent in a Strangers City

Voices of Waves

The One Who Lied

Maybe

The View

Stitches

Statues

Pink Ocean

Where I Use to be

Driving Away

He Was Really Expecting Me To Do It

When the Gates Are Locked

Drinking Rain

I am colorblind.
But I imagine colors like this:

I picture them to sing and dance,
To make friends and enemies.
To fall in love,
And then out.

It is these things I don't see,
When I look look my window,
To the painted world.

But even though I long to see the horizon,
And all it holds,
Like the mountains and forests,
And storm filled skies,
There is nothing I'd rather see
Then the color of my true loves eyes.

Mess of a Storm

I have seen
A glorious thing
Buried in the mess
Of a storm.

Within that hassle,
I shook the hand
Of the man
Who answers
Lost prayers.

He was gentle,
And forgiving.
He came with a song
That soothed the throbbing
Of a broken heart.

He is the voice
We all hear in our minds
Telling us to walk away
Or simply to just…
Breathe.

For only a moment
We talked.
And I learned so much.

For he knew what pain was.
And nor did he deny,
That it was temporary.

The Palace

Behind smiling eyes,
There is a war going on.
There are battles chosen,
And victories gained.
Even vital pieces are damaged,
Then lost.

But they never reach the palace of tears.
They never break its stonewall.
For the wall was built with rage,
And power.

The power to rise over every soldiers cry.

Dear Melissa

Dear Melissa,

At first,
The idea terrified me.
I saw it as a trap,
A prison,
With no safe way out.

From the outside,
It looked dangerous,
And volatile.

For to be in love,
Would to be defenseless.
It meant to be exposed,
And to be vulnerable to horrible pain.

It meant to be weak,
And powerless,
And probably miserable.

The idea seamed pointless.

Until I saw you.

When I saw you,

I fully understood why a man would give himself away.
I understood why a man would put his life on hold.
Why a man would chose to become unarmed,
And give up his independence.

I understood
Why a man would fall in love.

And with that one look at you,
I began to fall.
 As I watched you walk across the room,
I could feel myself begin to lose my balance.

Then I heard you laugh.
And it was like a hurricane came in,
And blew me into the deep darkness,
Where I could not see the light of where I was just seconds before.

For the light of you,
Glowed brighter then the sun at midday.

And now that I have you,
I couldn't imagine remembering life without you.
I can't bare the idea of sleeping alone,
Or spending another day afraid.

All I can see now is you.

All I can see is your hazel eyes,
Your sweet smile,
Your fervor and eagerness,
And your preciousness.

You are mine to protect.
And to defend.
And to content.

You are mine to love.

So that idea of a young me,
Terrified of falling in love,
Is a memory growing invisible in the taillights.

You are the reason I look forward to every tomorrow.

So dear Melissa,

Will you marry me?

Words of Wiseman

"I hate the man who taught me to love
For he disabled me
To live."

The Closing Cover

Once, I read a little boy a fairytale.
But he didn't listen.
It was a story of bravery;
How a young man saved his true love,
From a raging fire,
That threatened the tiny village,
That thrived in April.

I watched him walk back home
After my tale
And sighed;
Sad the he did not,
Like me,
See the brightness of its legend.

Ten years later,
I visited him again.

He did not remember me,
Nor why I wanted to see him.

As I watched him and listened,
I saw he lacked the strength of the prince,
The grace of the woman,
The courage of the knight,
And the love of a gentleman.

When the Deaf Sing

One day I woke up,
And my voice was gone.
I had lost it over night;
Misplaced it in my sleep.

Wherever it was,
It wasn't with me.
So I was silent.
All morning.
And all afternoon.

But in the evening,
I felt tugging on my fingers.
I looked down,
And it was my voice,
Resting in my hand.

It must have been there all day.
I just never noticed.

To the Man who Stole the Key

Now, it is as if I am chained to a door.
It is a way between two beings,
Belonging to either one.

I can see it,
Feel it,
Move it and touch it.
And even pass through it if I want.
But never all the way from one side to the other.
For I am stuck,
Where my wrist is locked.

I can freely move where I can,
Within my small, limited area.
But never beyond that.
For these binding chains,
Have always been holding me in this place.
Where I get a taste of both rooms,
Both worlds.
But only how they fix.
I watch people,
With greater strength from will,
Walk and wonder with bare arms.

They see me and mourn,
Because they feel sorry.
But only because they cannot help.
Or even speak out.
So I let them pass by.

How I wish I was one of them.

Run Faster than to Speak

There should have been a wall built there.
There should have been something
Put in place
Meant to hold me back.
Meant to prevent the damage
That comes with a flood.

Being happy during a freefall
Can make someone dangerous.
So forget what he said right now!
Before you remember to panic
And before you listen.

I am ready to be done.
To drive into that brick wall
And let it block me.

But the longer it runs from me
The more tired I become
And the hope of catching up
Runs away with it.

Every Day at 5

How many times the phone rings
Before you answer
Is what determines what I say.

If you pick up on the first ring
I will say hello
And leave it at that.

If you pick up on the second ring
I will ask you how your day was,
How your mother is,
And how you slept.

If you pick up on the third ring
I will ask you to come over
And maybe even stay the night.
All night.

If you pick up on the fourth ring
I will demand you tell me where you are,
Who you're with,
What you're doing,
And when you'll be home.

If you pick up on the fifth ring
I will be angry.
Furious and aggressive and fearless to tell you so.

If you pick up on the sixth ring
I will tell you that I love you
And that I want you

Forever and always.
And I'll beg you to stay with me.

If you pick up on the seventh ring
I will tell you that I never want to talk to you again
Or ever see you again.
I will walk out of your life
And move on.

And if you don't pick up,
I will try again tomorrow.

One Too Many Ships in the Ocean

If you sink my first ship,
I will be heartbroken
And upset
But congratulate you on your aim.

If you sink two of mine,
I will sink three of yours
And watch them fall to the bottom
And join mine.

But I know if I sink three of yours,
You will try for five of mine
For five is half my fleet,
Yet almost starting yours.

Then begins the Great War.
The sea becomes a blue battlefield.
We will fight,
But watch and cry
As all we have,
Swims below us,
And beneath us,
With them,
Their motivations will stay.

Eventually,
We will have no ships left.
It will just be me and you;
Treading water.

We will realize how foolish we had been,
And how hopeless we had become.

Only when we are defenseless,
Will we finally come together;
So as not to drown
In our own mistakes.

The Night I Spent in a Strangers City

When I stepped off the train,
It was midnight.
The buildings were strange,
And the people were stranger,
Yet friendly.

For as I walked,
They pointed me in the right direction.

The first place they pointed me to
Was a warehouse.

On the inside,
There were no walls.
There were high ceilings lined with white lights.

The floor of the building
Was a trampoline.

I played and had my youthful fun.
Even though at the time,
It did not occur to me,
That in order to jump,
There must have been a deep hole in the floor.

Naive to the idea,
I stayed there for an hour.

Then I stepped onto the street again.

The strangers pointed me towards a factory.

When I went inside,
The first room was a library.
It was quiet and calm.
Everyone in it was placid and tranquil.

I walked through noiselessly.

At the end of the library,
Was another door.

On the other side,
Was a movie theater.
It was packed full of teenagers,
With one seat left open in the front row,
For me.

I took it,
And the film started.

The things I saw,
Were unforgettable.

The things I saw were painful,
And amazing.
And lovely.
And terrifying.
And dramatic.

The things I saw,
Changed me.
When the credits finally rolled,

I looked over my shoulder,
To the rest of the theater.

And I was alone.

It floored me how forlorn I was.

When I eventually pulled myself to stand,
I walked back to the door I came in.

But instead of a library,
It was a rave.

It was a large dark, hot room
Full of jumping bodies,
And loud music and blinding strobe lights.

It sucked me into the middle,
Where I couldn't help
But dance with them.

I stayed in that factory,
Hot and happy for an hour
Until I found the back door,
That led outside.

Back on the streets,
I followed the stranger's directions.
They pointed,
This time,
To a church.

After climbing the enchanted steps
To the majestic stain glass door,
I walked through them,
To a coffee shop.

I sat there,
For a while,
And relaxed.

Then,
I walked to a door,
That looked like it lead to a kitchen.

But instead was a wedding,
In a striking chapel.

I did not realize it at first,
But I walked down the aisle,
As a bridesmaid,
Behind a few fellow women.

I lined up next to them,
In the steps before the alter,
And then turned to see the bride,
Walk her way to heaven.

I was in that building for an hour.

After the ceremony,
I slipped out a side door,
And stepped out onto the walkway once more.

The next place they pointed to,

Was a grand bank.

The hour I spent in there,
Was the most exhausting,
Of my life.

For on the inside,
Was a daycare,
Where I alone,
Was responsible,
For feeding a total of fifty.

After the little angels
Were fed and asleep,
I left.

The walk to the next building however,
Was lengthy,
And very tiring.

My feet ached once I reached its gates.

It was a prison.

On the inside,
Abandoned as it was,
Was so,
So dark.

I chose now,
Not to remember that lonely hour.
For I know it would haunt me.

I was so relived to leave.

The next walk,
Was not as far.
The strangers pointed me,
Still in this strange city,
To a town house.

A simple,
Happy looking one.
With light brick walls,
And flower beds on the windowsills,
Alive and vibrant.

I sauntered up the stone porch,
And through the honey sweet wooden door.

The inside walls,
Were lined with hundreds of photos.
I took my time to look at the faces of the family,
The lucky family, as they grew.

After an hour of reminiscing,
Longing for what they had,
I left.

Ready for my next intrigue.

The next time,
They people led me to a greenhouse.

After I strolled in,

And closed the door behind me,
The room was full of sunlight,
As if it was noon.

Roses.
Lilies.
Sunflowers.

All so delicate and handsome.

But as I took my first step forwards,
I came to find chains,
Binding my wrists and ankles.
So the sixty minutes I was there,
I was only able to stay still and only look.

Any attempt to move,
Was so painful.
Possible,
But painful.

Then it was once again,
Time to go.
Gladly this time.

On the sidewalk,
My wrists and ankles were no longer chained.

I was then guided to a park,
Where I sat and watched children play,
Unsurprised,
From the dark.
I watched a girl,

Walk towards a boy who was on the swings.

I wanted to go to her,
And tell her it was dangerous,
But I could not.

I knew she must learn for herself.

So I just watched
And prayed for her and her bruises.

Then,
I was led to a building

A hospital this time.

On the inside,
They put me in a bed,
In a quiet room,
With no one but the beeping from a machine,
To keep me company.
For the entire hour.

Never before had I been so…
So…
So…

The last place,
Was a courthouse.

I knew what to do.

I proceeded inside,
And stood in front of the judge's place,
In the middle of the room,
And waited.

As I waited,
I remembered all the other buildings.

The warehouse,
Where I played.
The factory,
With the library,
The movie,
And the rave.

The church,
With the coffee shop,
And luxurious wedding.

The bank,
With all the little ones.

The prison.

The town house,
So calm and sweet.

The greenhouse,
Where I was chained.

The park,
Where I could only watch.

The hospital,
Where I waited.

And then I stood before the judge
My maker,
To know my way.

When my final hour was up,
I turned and walked away.

I then left the city,
The same way I came.

I slept on the train,
But somehow,
Ended up okay.

I will never again be scared of strange places,
Because I know at dawn,
The train will take me home.

Voices of Waves

Coming back from the sea,
I tried to remember my name,
But the waves must have washed it away.
I tried to remember who you were,
But that must have drowned,
When I dived.
I tried to remember what I was here to do,
But it must have gone with the tide.
I tried to remember a time before I saw the sun,
But that must have been gone since I was very small.
For the time before the sea,
Was dark.
I shield it from my voice,
And from my mind,
Just in case the ocean doesn't remember me.

The One Who Lied

The demon on my shoulder tells me to love you.
He tells me you are what I've been looking for,
What I see
And what I feel.
I can even fell in myself,
This strong will to love you.
Yet he was the one,
Who yells to be late,
To lie,
To run and hide,
And to jump in front of bullets.
He is the one who gets me in trouble.
It's his brother,
Who tells me to be good.
Yet,
I cannot hear him.
I cannot tell if he chooses to be silent,
Or if I simply cannot hear him,
Over the sound of his dark twin's voice.
In which case,
There is nothing more to do.
Nothing more that can be said,
I will do as the demon pleases,
And I shall love you.
And his brother will watch me fall,
Deeper and deeper in vain.
For in case the demon loses his balance,
And falls,
Unable to regain strength,
I will be too deep in love to find my way out.

Maybe

And then I thought to myself;
Maybe I'm asleep.
Maybe I'm day dreaming.
Maybe I'm in a movie.
Maybe my love is at my door.
Maybe I'm going.
Or maybe I'm already gone.
It was thoughts like these that keep me running,
Even though I know I'm heading into a more difficult path of greens.
But I keep running,
With knowing that,
In case the great become lesser than me,
I will be just over their heads.

The View

The optimistic one,
Would say the glass is half full.
The pessimistic one,
Of course,
Would say it's half empty.

Both sides are true.
But due to the perspective they were seen as.

But what if…

The glass represents was not an easy task;
But something terrible.
For if you said the glass represented something like poison,
The views would be switched.

The optimistic one,
Would say it's half empty,
And would still be looking at the brighter side.
As the glass was half full of nothing,
Rather than poison.

And the pessimistic one would see it as half full.
Only seeing the value of the poison
That is actually contained.

So it would be smart not to judge
When one said the glass is half empty.

They might be the brighter one.

Stitches

Back then,
There were pieces of me all over the world.

Part of me at the bottom of the vast ocean.
Part of me hiding from the blinding sun,
In the gloomy shade,
Or under a hideous wild tree.
Part of me drying up in the eternal desert,
Lost and hopeless.
Another part in the paradise of the other,
Washing itself away in the wind of the arctic.

Part of me sorted in the back of my closet.
Another part under the lonely bed.
More in boxes locked in the basement,
Like Christmas ornaments or china.

And tiny parts falling from the sky with the rain,
Landing miles away from each other,
And then wandering in different directions.

But a very small piece was closed with me.
And I lived,
Always in fear,
That that piece would run away too.

And when it did,

You caught me so easily.
So I stayed there,
In your arms.

Ever since then,
I haven't moved.
But all those pieces of me,
Found there way back to each other.
And eventually back to me.

You used your magic like stitches on me.
And I'm covered in scars and bruises
But now,
I'm still beating.
Still breathing.
And it's your breath I breathe.

Statues

Life as a statue would be boring.
Especially if you were inside.

If you were outside,
It would be so much easier to watch the world.

If you were colorful,
You could be famous.
People would pose by you and take pictures.
You could be on the Internet,
Or posted on posters.
And people would know your name.

But you could never move.
Your eyes set in stone.

If only you could take one step,
Just one step forward,

That would be all it would take.

Pink Ocean

The day has saved its sweetest,
And it knows,
For the beginning of the end.
It has been soaking in the breath of roses.

He loves me…

Ready till this moment,
To furnish us,
Vibrantly kiss,
And stain the grass.

He loves me not…

For its rays are oceans,
An ocean of renaissance
Waiting in May,
For the gold to settle,
Deep,
Pure and dire.

He loves me…

Where I Use to Be

It used to be his face,
I'd see before I fell asleep.

It used to be his heavenly voice,
That sang me the precious lullaby.

It used to be his hands,
I'd feel on my skin.

I wish I could go back to that now.

It's still his face,
I see before I fall asleep.

I still hear the ring of his voice,
Telling me it's over.

And I still feel the ghost of his hands,
Where they use to be.

And I still feel the ice of his lips,
Where they left mine.

Driving Away

One of these days,
I will look at you,
For the last time.
That thought is scary,
But I'm ready now.

I've loved the time,
I have spent with you.
It has made me so strong,
And I will look back,
Knowing I made my mark on you as well.

Yet I still look out my window,
And think to myself,

"Someday,
I will drive away from here
And never
Ever
Look back."

He Was Really Expecting Me To Do It

"Are you serious?" I asked him.

"Absolutely" he said. "I definitely want you to do this."

"If you are sure…" I murmured under my breath as I looked at the giant pile of hay next to me. It was at least six feet high and had the width of a living room. And somewhere inside of it, he insisted, was a needle I was in charge of finding.

"You better get started he said." And then got in his truck and drove away.

I watched him disappear into the dust in disbelief. He was really expecting me to do it; to find a needle in a hay stack.

There was a slight breeze blowing over the field I stood in. it caused some of the loose strands of hay to fly off of the top of the stack and annoyingly brush against my face. I swore.

And then after I did that, I began to kick the heaving pile of hay out of anger. I kicked and writhed until my feet and shins were sore. Because never once in my life did I ever expect to be put in such a God-awful terrible place like this.

After my fit, I came to realize that I would be stuck there until I found that needle. So then began the longest and hungriest five days of my life. When I was finally over, I had realized that I in fact came across the needle several times before I realized what it was. I didn't care though.

When he drove up that fifth evening to pick me up, my clothes were torn and my gut was empty. As was my heart. He had apples in the truck when I climbed in and then put the needle in his outstretched hand.

He looked at his, turning it through his fingers.

"Very good." he said "Now I will take you home."

Then I woke up.

When the Gates Are Locked

It's hard to believe that everyone who spoke up is wrong. No matter how much I wish they were right, I knew I had to accept it.

I knew the cancer was there. It was there for most of my life and I always knew it was certain so when it finally took me, I was ready to die. I had taken advantage of the twenty four years I had to live and made them the best they could be.

Death was no surprise.

The real surprise is… that I am still here.

The world's big misconception is, is that when a person body dies, so does their mind. But that is not true.

My body is broken; it does not work. It has lost communication to my brain but my brain has not lost communication to itself.

So, I can still think. I can still remember my life and everything in it. Who I am, who I knew, where I lived and everything I did or said. I can recall the memories pure as day.

But I can't see, hear, feel, taste or speak.

I am trapped in here, somewhere, forever and can only think.

Everyone who has ever died in the world is still somewhere, fixed in their own mind. Just like me.

The idea of staying this way forever was petrifying. I wish that I am not alone; that I at least had a little bit of heaven or earth.

As I thought about that, being somewhere between heaven and earth, I realized where I was.

I was in hell.

Hell was not far away from earth. As a matter of fact, it was extremely close.

It was right under my feet for twenty four years.

If only they knew how close it was.

This place I am in now is a white space where I can't move or breathe, but my mind is wired so strongly that my own voices in my head can't drown each other out.

* * *

Up until they buried me, I had my memory.

I watched the days of my life and remembered all the different people and places.

But since I can no longer sleep, I can no longer store those memories so they slowly faded.

And I was alone with my consciousness.

Not long after, the other voices came. I didn't know who they were or where they came from.

They spoke to me, insulted me and affronted me.

Eventually I became insane.

And my own voice blended with those around me, screaming into the ground.

Made in the USA
Lexington, KY
09 March 2016